CONNECT WITH ANYONE

How to Be Instantly Likeable, Irresistibly Charming,
and Quickly Connect with People On a Deep Level

CONNECT WITH ANYONE
How to Be Instantly Likeable, Irresistibly Charming,
and Quickly Connect with People On a Deep Level
Copyright © 2017 by Dominic Mann

CONNECT WITH ANYONE

How to Be Instantly Likeable, Irresistibly Charming,
and Quickly Connect with People On a Deep Level

By
Dominic Mann

TABLE OF CONTENTS

INTRODUCTION

I know something.

I have a dirty little secret.

And it's about you.

But I'll tell you if you want. Because I'm a nice guy like that.

Are you ready for this?

You want to impress someone.

There, I said it. Groundbreaking, right? Chances are that no matter who you are, there's someone else out there that you feel the need to impress. That's just the way humans work.

Everyone wants to impress someone.

And a lot of people want to impress *everyone.*

The problem?

People are idiots. They go around trying to be impressive, but they do it in the worst possible ways. They think that if they're attractive enough, or successful enough, or rich enough…THEN people will be impressed. THEN they'll have killer social lives.

But such is not the case.

In fact, believing that you need to be tangibly impressive in order to impress someone will just kill your self-esteem and leave you damaged and insecure. And it will prevent you from being your true self. You'll be forced to put on a show and a constant smile, rather than letting your true personality shine through.

So yeah.

Not a good idea.

But unfortunately, far too many people have already fallen into that trap, and aren't even aware of it. They know something's wrong with their social life, but they're not exactly sure how to fix it.

And the result of falling into this trap? A bunch of flimsy, broken, surface-level relationships with people who don't really care about you.

Very few people in this world are capable of making those deep, human connections that we all naturally yearn for. Very few people know how to dive beneath the surface of a relationship and truly *connect* with a person.

That's why I wrote this book.

This book will show you how to connect with people in deep and meaningful ways. (And impress the heck out of them in the process.)

Because if there's one thing I absolutely KNOW about people, it's that they want to feel connected to *something*. In fact, I'd go so far as to say that they *need* to feel connected to something. And that something can be you.

But you need to go about it the right way.

This is the right way.

Enjoy…

CHAPTER 1:
IT'S ALL ABOUT THEM

I want you to close your eyes for a moment.

Actually, wait, no. Sorry. That wouldn't work. I just realized you can't keep reading with your eyes closed.

Okay. Let's just pretend that you closed your eyes.

Now, with your eyes closed, let's use our imaginations.

I want you to think about the last time you first met someone that you were super attracted to. Imagine every little detail. Where you are, what you're doing, what it smells like.

Now think about how you acted. Think about how aware you were of every little thing. Think about how conscious you were of the way you were standing or sitting or whatever. Think about how aware you were of how your breath smelled, and how your hair was combed, and every single other possible thing.

Now think about the conversation you had with this person.

Think about how you tried to build yourself up. Think about how you tried to come off as impressive as possible.

Now think about how big of a failure you are.

Because you did everything wrong.

Freaking idiot.

WHERE MOST PEOPLE GO WRONG

Sorry, I shouldn't have called you an idiot.

I'm the idiot.

But that doesn't change the fact that most people are absolutely horrible at flirting and connecting with people and first impressions and all of that crap.

And maybe you're good at it. Maybe you totally nailed your last flirtatious encounter.

But probably you didn't. And I just say that because you're a person, and as a general rule of thumb, people are horrible at flirting.

Because here's the thing: people are naturally self-centered. Right? Everyone is at the center of their own universe.

Sometimes that's a good thing. Most of the time it's not.

If you're seeking to impress and connect with someone, you need to put them at the center of your universe.

This is the most important thing that we're going to discuss in this entire book.

If you want to connect with someone, you need to put 100% of your focus on them. This is absolutely the most critical change you could ever make to improve your social skills.

Stop trying to build yourself up. Stop trying to make yourself look cool. Stop trying to be impressive. Stop constantly fixing your hair and worrying about that zit on your chin. Don't worry about yourself at all.

Instead, invest every ounce of your attention in the other person.

If you're truly trying to impress someone, they deserve 100% of your attention. And if you can give them that...then you're already well on your way to successfully connecting with them.

IMPRESS BY BEING IMPRESSED

I've been on a lot of dates.

I'm not trying to brag or anything. And even if I was, I'm not sure that this would be effective bragging. Because not only have I been on a lot of dates, I've been on probably TOO MANY dates. There's a point where the number of dates a person has been on stops being impressive, and begins to be frightening. I'm probably on the frightening end of the spectrum.

I've been on about 50 dates in the last year. With 50 different girls. And yeah, before you beat me to it, I'm aware that I might seem like a little bit of a man-ho. Or maybe I just seem really desperate. Oh well. Whatever. Deal with it.

Anyways, that's not the point.

The point is that I've been on a lot of dates. And usually when I'm on these dates, I try really hard to impress whoever I'm with. Which makes sense, right? Dates are like job interviews. You want to highlight all of your strengths and come off as impressive as possible...because then you might get a job. Of one kind or another. Ahem.

But overtime, I've started to notice a recurring pattern: if you really want to impress someone, then be impressed by them.

People love to feel impressive. So if you make someone feel impressive when they're around you, they'll love being around you. You'll have an instant friend forever. And you'll be able to connect with them in a way that most people simply can't.

I'm telling you. It seems super simple, but it's SOOOO effective. The most impressive thing you could ever do is to be impressed by whoever you're with.

If you're trying to connect with someone (in any situation, not just on a date) focus completely on making them feel as important and impressive as possible. The more you focus on them, the more they'll like you.

It's as simple as that.

BALANCE IN ALL THINGS

Really quick, I just want to take a step back.

It's important to point out that it's possible to take this whole "focus completely on the other person" thing a little bit too far. You need to remember that there's a balance to everything.

While you shouldn't obsess over yourself (as most people tend to do when they're trying to be impressive) you should still be a person. A good person, preferably. It's okay to talk and tell stories of your own. It's okay to maintain basic human hygiene and not be a totally disgusting slob. It's okay to give your personality a chance to shine. Just don't prioritize that above helping the other person's personality shine.

The more you focus on the other person, the more impressive you'll be and the more meaningful of a connection you'll be able to make. Up to a certain point. Just remember balance.

CHAPTER 2:
GET THEM TO MAKE YOU LAUGH

Laughter is the key to everything.

It can unlock doors that would otherwise be sealed shut forever.

Heck, it can unlock doors that you didn't even know existed. Laughter is so, so powerful. And I'm a huge fan of it. It can help you connect with another person on a far deeper level than most people realize. Laughter breaks down barriers and opens hearts.

Unfortunately, laughter is on the endangered species list. It's dying out, slowly but surely.

Consider this statistic: the average kid laughs 300 times per day. The average adult laughs 5.

I'm no expert, but that seems like a pretty sucky trend to me. When a number starts out that big and ends up so small…something is wrong.

Luckily for ya'll, I'm super amazing and have cracked the code to successfully using laughter in any social interaction. But you have to go about it in a different way than you're probably thinking of…

HUMOR: YOUR SECRET WEAPON

Being funny is great.

If I'm on a date and I can get the girl to laugh out loud within 30 seconds of picking her up…then I know it's going to be a good date. I've never been on a bad date that started with a laugh. And I've rarely been on a good date that didn't.

By no means would I consider myself an extraordinarily funny person. But I'm probably slightly above average. Not trying to brag or anything, just stating a fact. I can generally get people to laugh. Not always on the first try, but if you're desperate enough, eventually you'll get a pity laugh at the very least.

And actually, last year I somehow got the opportunity to go and perform live stand-up comedy in front of several hundred people. And let me tell you, there is no better feeling in the entire world than to have someone totally lose their crap over one of your jokes.

When I did stand-up comedy, I made a good portion of the audience cry from laughter. And I couldn't believe how amazing it felt. Humor is like mind-control. Or hypnosis. People lost control of their bodily functions simply because of the words that were coming out of my mouth.

And I loved it.

Making someone else laugh is the best feeling in the world. Everyone loves to be funny.

And here's the good news: you can make that dream come true for another person. If you truly want to connect with someone, there's something you can do that's even better than being funny. Get them to be funny.

Rather than be funny yourself, try to make whoever you're with feel funny. If you can successfully do that, they'll instantly love you forever. I can absolutely guarantee that. It works every single time.

FAKE IT TILL YOU MAKE IT

Some people are naturally funny. It will be easy to find genuinely funny things to laugh at. They'll make this technique easy for you.

Some people are NOT naturally funny. It will be super, super hard to find genuinely funny things to laugh at. They'll make this technique a friggin' pain in the butt for you.

But it's important to remember that EVERYONE is capable of being funny. Everyone. Some people will make it easier than others, but everyone has the potential. You have to believe that in order for this technique to work. You have to believe that everyone is absolutely hilarious.

Make it a habit to expect every single person you meet to be hilarious.

It kinda weird, but people tend to act the way that you expect them to.

If you see someone and you expect them to be super shy and lame and boring...chances are that's how they'll act. Or at least, that's all you'll see. (Humans are notoriously good at only seeing the things they want to.)

However, on the other end of the spectrum, if you expect someone to be super awesome and hilarious...they'll almost always live up to your expectations. Eventually. Sometimes you have to fake it till you make it, so to speak. Sometimes you'll really have to use your imagination to believe that someone is capable of being funny.

And you know what, maybe every once in awhile someone will let you down. But that'll be the exception to the rule. For the most part, if you expect someone to be funny…then they'll be funny.

It's pretty amazing, actually.

I'm sure someone out there has done a study about why people tend to act the way they're expected to. I'm sure there's some sort of totally epic scientific theory that would explain why this happens.

I don't have that. I don't know why this happens. But it does.

Chances are you've seen it happen yourself over and over again. Have you ever noticed how you tend to act differently around different sets of friends? Again, I don't know why, but people are really good at falling into character and acting the way people expect them to.

And you can use this to your advantage. Expect every person you meet to be the coolest, most hilarious person ever. And treat them like that. And they'll love you. I can guarantee it.

BE GENUINE

Making someone feel hilarious is one of the most effective ways to win their love. As we established earlier, everyone loves to feel hilarious.

But it's important that you go about this in the right way. You need to be genuine.

Don't fake laugh. People can tell when you're fake laughing. And it's horrible. It'll instantly negate all of the positive effects of laughing. No matter how tempted you might be, don't fake laugh. It's not worth it.

Only laugh at the things that you think are actually funny.

Now, this poses a bit of a problem, right? Because what about the people who just aren't funny at all? And what about the people that have absolutely terrible senses of humor that you simply can't understand? How can you genuinely laugh at those people and make them feel impressive and funny?

Well, there is a bit of good news. Chances are, if you're trying super hard to find humor in something…you'll find it. Or even if a joke that someone tells is absolutely terrible and not funny at all, maybe you can find something funny in your current situation. Or maybe you can think about a hilarious experience that you had recently. Or maybe you can think about the funniest line from your favorite comedy movie.

Honestly, it doesn't really matter why you're laughing or what you're laughing at. As long as you're genuinely laughing, it'll have the effect you're looking for.

But don't fake laugh. That's just cheap.

CHAPTER 3:
IDENTIFY THEIR PASSIONS

Okay, I have a really quick question for you.

However, this time, there's no need to close your eyes. This is a pretty simple question.

What is something that you absolutely *love*?

What's something that you're so passionate about, you could do it every day for the rest of your life and never get bored? What's something that you love so much you could talk about it for hours without realizing where the time went?

Everyone has something like this.

For me, it's definitely stand-up comedy. And self-help.

But chances are that it's going to be different for you.

Maybe it's food. Maybe it's running. Maybe it's sports. Maybe it's stocks. Maybe it's video games. Maybe it's my books.

Whatever it is that you absolutely love, I want you to take a second to think about it. Think about how much you love it.

Now think about how awesome it would be if you had someone that loved that thing just as much. Think about how well you guys would "click".

Think about how you could just talk and talk and talk and never get bored.

That would be pretty epic, right?

Well, what if I told you that you could make that dream come true for someone else?

YOU DON'T MATTER

I want you to take a second to fully absorb the meaning of this section title.

It's kind of funny, but this seems to be a bit of a recurring theme throughout this book.

You don't matter.

And while that's not entirely true, it is mostly true. When you're trying to impress someone, you don't matter at all. If you want to truly connect, you need to be entirely focused on them.

This is a really hard habit to master. It's going to feel really weird the first couple of times you try it. It's definitely going to take some practice to master.

But it's worth it.

When you stop trying to be impressive and start being impressed, your overall "impressiveness" will shoot way up. It's counterintuitive, but it works. Every time.

So next time you meet someone that you really want to connect with…don't try to impress them. Forget about your passions. At least for a little while. Obviously no relationship will work if it's completely one-sided, in either direction. It's important to have your own personality, and it's certainly okay to have your own passions.

But when you're first trying to connect with someone, pretend like they're the only person in the whole entire world that matters. Focus all of your efforts on identifying and exploring the other person's passions.

If they're passionate about something…then you're passionate about it. Be the person that you could lose track of time with, and talk to for hours on end.

EVERYONE HAS A PASSION

Every single person on this planet is passionate about at least one thing.

Whenever you meet someone, your job is to find that one thing. Because if you can…oh boy. That's your golden ticket. It'll impress them beyond all amazement and allow you to connect with them on a much deeper level than most people.

If that sounds super amazing and hyped up…that's because it *is* super amazing.

Talking to another person about the thing that they're most passionate about is one of the coolest experiences ever. It's so cool to see people open up and get super enthusiastic and animated over something. Especially since so many people in our society today are so reserved and timid in public.

And the awesome thing is that *literally everyone* has something that they're super passionate about. Even if it's something you might find boring, like puzzles or video games or celebrity gossip.

And every single person you see or interact with every day has a passion. Never doubt that. Everyone has a passion.

Right now, as I'm typing these words, I'm sitting in my local public library. There are plenty of people all around me. And I don't know a single one of them. They're total strangers. But if I had a little cheat sheet that told me what each person's "one thing" was…I could instantly connect with anyone in this room.

I'm telling you, this technique is freaking *powerful*.

Unfortunately, real life doesn't give you a cheat sheet. Real life is a little bit harder. You have to do a little bit of digging. But it is totally possible. I've never ever met a single person that didn't have a passion they weren't willing to talk about.

Your job is to figure out what that passion is.

IT TAKES WORK

People absolutely adore small talk.

And it drives me insane.

I swear, at least 90% of the conversations I hear or am a part of everyday never make it past the small talk barrier. People just talk about the same dumb things overs and over again.

"Oh, hey, how are you doing today?"

"Pretty good, how about yourself?"

"Oh, you know. Not too bad."

"Cool. Well, hey, I'll see you around."

"Oh yeah, you too. Have a nice day."

That is probably the most common conversation I've ever heard in my entire life. And I'm sure you've heard it too. It happens dozens of times a day, all around you, all the time.

If you want to truly connect with people and talk to them about their passions, you're going to have to jump beyond your average small talk. You'll need to dive deep. You'll need to dig around a little bit.

It won't be easy. I want to be very upfront about that. There's a reason small talk is a thing. It's easy. It takes almost no thought or effort. It allows people to connect in small ways without a significant investment.

If you want to move beyond small talk, it'll take some work. It'll certainly be hard the first couple of times.

But if you're willing to put in the effort, the rewards are astronomical. You'll be able to connect with ANYONE. Which is definitely one of the most valuable talents a person is capable of possessing.

Now for a personal story...

I have a lady friend. That may come as a surprise to some of you, but it's true. I like a girl and she likes me. Shocker.

I've been hanging out with her family a lot recently, and it's been great. Not nearly as awkward as *Meet the Parents* led me to believe. I get along great with all of her siblings, and her mom absolutely adores me.

But for some reason I was having a hard time connecting with her dad. He didn't dislike me, but he didn't really like me either. I was just a person that existed, and I was on the very outskirts of his radar. I almost didn't exist to him.

I tried and tried to connect with him in all sorts of ways, but then I realized I wasn't following my own advice. I was trying to show off and be impressive in my own way. I was focusing on me. Not him.

So a couple of weeks ago I decided to stop being a freaking idiot. I was going to stop trying to impress him. And instead, I was going to focus 100% of my efforts on trying to learn more about him.

One day I was helping him out with some yardwork, and I decided this would be the perfect opportunity to jump beyond small talk and figure out what he was actually passionate about.

As I suspected, it wasn't easy. It took some digging. And some educated guesswork. But eventually I got through to him when we started talking about fishing. Which led to a conversation about camping, and slot canyons, and rappelling. And for some weird reason, we also talked a lot about butternut squash. Not really sure why.

But those were all things that he absolutely LOVED. And it was so cool to see him come alive as we talked about his passions. He'd always been pretty shy and reserved, but as soon as we started talking about something he really cared about, he became animated an enthusiastic. It was super neat.

And once I got him going, I barely had to do any of the talking. I just had to sit back and relax and watch as our relationship improved by the second.

I was able to connect with him on a meaningful level that day, and things have been great ever since then. Every time I see him he'll smile and initiate a conversation with me. He's not shy anymore. I struck gold.

I'm telling you, this thing is like magic. It blows me away every time. Unearthing a person's passions is a guaranteed way to get them to love you.

Ooh, and one more thing about this story that's important to understand: I wasn't passionate about his passions. But that didn't prevent me from taking the time to talk about them and be interested in what he was saying.

Your job isn't to be passionate about everything. Your job is to identify what somebody is passionate about, and then talk to them about it. That's it. Even if you're not super passionate about something, you can still be interested in it.

However, you should never fake passion. As we discussed in an earlier chapter, it's important to be genuine. Don't pretend to love something that you don't. You shouldn't ever feel like you need to change your opinions just to fit in and be accepted by another person.

That's one thing that I've noticed on all the dates that I've been on. People have a really hard time taking a stand and holding true to their own opinions. They'll follow along with just about anything if they think it will help them fit in.

And I'm guilty of the same thing. If I'm with someone that I care about and they're talking about how much they loved a certain movie, I'll usually agree with them, even if I hated the movie. You've probably done something similar at one point or another in your life.

Don't be like that.

Don't pretend to like things that you don't. However, there's a big difference between "liking" something and being "interested" in something.

It's very important to distinguish between those two things. I don't want you to pretend to be passionate about everything. That's cheap. But you CAN be interested in everything. Sure, some things are easier to be interested in than others. But if you try hard enough, you can find something interesting in just about everything.

And as you take interest in the passions of others, it'll do wonders for your social life. I can absolutely promise you that.

CHAPTER 4:
DON'T SHY AWAY FROM BOLDNESS

You're super lame.

Man, I'm great at starting chapters, aren't I?

I should really consider becoming a politician. I feel like a lot of my skill sets would transfer over.

Anyways. That's not the point. Sorry.

The point is that you're super lame.

Well, not you specifically. But just people in general. People are lame. Always.

Seriously, when was the last time you had a super awesome interaction with a stranger?

Go ahead, take all the time you need. I'll wait. When was the last time a stranger totally made your day?

Unless you live in Portland where you're constantly knee-deep in hippies, chances are that most of the people you meet are quite boring. That's just the way things are. People are boring and lame and shy and reserved and afraid to let their true personalities shine.

If you want to become more interesting and impressive, you need to stop being lame like everyone else. And in order for that to happen, you're going to have to do something very, very hard.

You're going to have to be bold.

YOU NEED TO BE DIFFERENT

So many people strive so hard to be normal. So many people want nothing more than to just "fit in". And I'm not really sure why. It doesn't make a ton of sense to me.

Because here's the deal. If you want to truly connect with people, you need to completely ditch that mindset. Normal people are boring. There are plenty of people out there that do a great job "fitting in". You're not one of those people.

You need to be unabashedly bold and unique.

Don't try to be normal. Instead, try to be different. All the time. In everything you do.

People are never going to remember a normal person. People are only going to remember you if you give them something to remember you by. You need to be bold. You need to do the things that normally you wouldn't dare to do.

Now, obviously there's a balance to everything.

I'm not telling you that you should just go all out crazy. There are plenty of crazy people out there in the world. And we certainly don't need anymore.

But don't be afraid to be spontaneous. Don't be afraid to be your true self.

I used to be super lame during social interactions. I'd think of things that I could say or do, but I'd be too worried about standing out. So I never did any of those things. I kept them inside my head, where they couldn't make any sort of a difference.

But eventually I just gave up on the whole "try to be normal and socially acceptable" thing. I decided to become more bold in the things I said and did. And the results were rather surprising. My social life skyrocketed. It turns out that people love people that are bold enough to be themselves. Who woulda thunk.

But seriously, as I started to say the things I wanted to say, regardless of how it might be perceived, people started to respect me.

You can do the same thing for your own social life.

But the important thing to remember is to start small. Don't go all out all at once. I see people do this all the time, and they fail miserably. Not just with this technique, but with any technique. You need to start small and work your way up.

Here's how I'd recommend getting started with this technique...

DITCH THE SMALL TALK (MOSTLY)

I know we already talked about this a little bit.

Let's talk about it a bit more.

I've already established my burning, passionate hatred for small talk, right?

It's absolutely THE WORST. I hate it.

Sure, it exists for a reason. Sometimes it's helpful. But at least 90% of the time small talk is such a stupid waste of time. You could be using the same number of words to connect with someone on a much deeper and more meaningful level.

So that's my first "Bold Challenge" for you. Don't be afraid to be bold in the way you start conversations. Ditch the small talk. And go right for the big stuff.

That's how I met my aforementioned lady friend. I sat down next to her at a talent show thingy-ma-bobber and the first thing I said to her was: "So. What's your favorite thing about life?"

That single question launched one of the most interesting discussions I've ever had with another human being. I had the time of my life.

And the rest, as they say, is history.

Next time you start a conversation, don't just say "how was your day?" or "how're you doing?". Ask something really deep and unusual and bold.

You can steal my "what's your favorite thing about life?" question if you want. Who knows, it might get you a totally kick-butt girlfriend. Here are a couple of my other favorite ways to start conversations:

- If you had to rate your life on a scale of 1-10, overall, what would it be?
- If you were on the run from the law, where would you go?
- What color is your toothbrush? What does that say about your personality?

- What's one thing you've always wanted to try, but never have?
- What's the most embarrassing thing that has ever happened to you?

That last one is really great at breaking the ice and getting through to people that are a little too formal and reserved. It almost always leads to hilarious stories that are a lot of fun and inspire plenty of laughter.

Actually, now that I think about it, that question is probably a great way to implement the advice from Chapter Two. It's practically a foolproof way to get a funny story out of someone. And if you can get someone to tell you a funny story, you're in a prime position to laugh your guts out and make them feel hilarious. And then they'll love you forever.

You're welcome.

Anyways. The point is that you should never start a conversation "normally" ever again. Normal conversations are so boring. Be bold. Ask weird questions. Pretty much every single amazing conversation that I've ever had with someone started with a funky question.

Sure, it was kinda scary the first couple of times. But it's so worth it. I'm telling you.

And really quick, before we move on, I just wanted to let you guys know about a little resource that has really helped me a lot: https://www.youtube.com/watch?v=WDbxqM4Oy1Y

That's a link to a totally amazing TED talk. It's seriously one of my all-time favorites. Which is saying a lot. Because TED talks are amazing. I actually like to start my day by listening to a couple of TED talks, because they fire my brain up and get me thinking outside the box.

The above TED talk is all about a concept called "big talk". It's super inspiring, and will hopefully give you some good advice and help you incorporate the technique in this chapter in your daily life.

You should all watch it. Right now. And if you don't, you're a loser.

Cool?

Cool.

BE THE PERFECT VERSION OF YOURSELF

This is a little hack that has really helped me to ditch my sense of "normalcy" and fully embrace my bold side.

We all have this idea in the back of our mind of what the perfect version of ourselves would be like.

Ultra-fit, incredibly rich, hilarious, wise, cool under pressure, a long-term thinker, excellent at every game you play, etc, etc.

Right?

That's a generalization, but most people want something along those lines. Everyone wants to be the perfect person. Well, not everyone. We all know that one guy whose life is going to complete crap and he just doesn't care. But oh well. He'll probably OD and die soon, so who cares. Other than his dealer. Obviously.

But anyways, my point is that most of us have a general concept of the person we wish we were.

What if I told you I found a pretty handy way to access this perfect version of yourself?

Well, lucky for you, I'm a freaking brilliant genius.

Next time you enter a social setting, just ask yourself the following question: what would the perfect version of myself do right now?

And then do whatever you come up with.

Now, of course, you won't actually be perfect. But you'll be a heck of a lot closer than you would be otherwise.

It's weird, but asking this one simple question helps me a lot. And not just in social settings, but in life in general. When I think about what the perfect version of myself would do, I'm much more likely to make the right decision.

Here's an example: I was out of town for a little while and just got back this evening. I almost always workout from 3-4pm every single day, but I missed today because I was on the road. And when I got home I told myself "hey, I'm a relatively fit dude. I workout every day. Missing just one day won't hurt. I went yesterday, and I'll go tomorrow. No biggie."

I rationalized skipping my workout to the point that I didn't even feel guilty doing it. I honestly thought it would be just fine to skip today.

But then I asked myself: "what would the perfect version of myself" do?

And the answer was obvious. Go to the gym.

So I went.

And it was great. I smiled at the lady at the front desk, played a couple of games of pick-up basketball, made some new friends. And none of that would've happened if I'd been my normal self.

And the really awesome thing is that this exercise can be applied to just about any area of life. It's super simple, super effective, and surprisingly fun.

And if you're not totally convinced that you'll love it, just ask yourself… would the perfect version of yourself try this experiment?

Boom. I just inception-ized this sucker. I always knew I was the next Christopher Nolan. Watch out Oscars. Just wait till I turn my talents towards the big screen…

Haha, just kidding. But in all seriousness, this technique has helped me connect with people in ways that I wouldn't be able to otherwise. It helps me to get out of my comfort zone and to be bolder than I normally would be. It's completely revolutionized my social life. And I'm positive it can do the same thing for you.

Give it a shot. You won't be disappointed.

And if you are…well screw you. The perfect version of yourself wouldn't be disappointed.

You gotta step up your game, homie.

CONCLUSION

Well here we are.

The end of the book.

Hopefully it's been an enjoyable reading experience. I always try my best to be as helpful as possible while keeping things fun and conversational. I'm sure some people hate my writing style, but I suppose you must have at least found it tolerable if you made it all the way to the conclusion.

If you have in fact enjoyed yourself, I hope you'll do me a favor and review this book. Reviews are the lifeblood of book sales. And book sales are the lifeblood of my bank account. And my bank account is the lifeblood of my relationship with my girlfriend. And my girlfriend does Jiu Jitsu. You don't want to upset her. She'll kick your butt any day of the week.

Although, now that I think about it, there's actually something you could do that would make me so much happier than any review ever could. The thing I want more than anything else is for you to take action on what you've learned in this book.

We've covered a lot of different techniques to impress and connect with people. Use them.

You'd be surprised at how many people will read a book and then never take action on anything they learn. It's ridiculous. I almost feel guilty making so much money off of my books. I may be a little bit biased, but I tend to believe that my books have great information. But I know that the vast majority of people won't take advantage of that information.

Don't be one of those people. Don't be an idiot. Use the things that you've been reading about. Today. If you procrastinate, you'll be even less likely to use them. Get out of the house right now and go have a conversation with a total stranger. Use as many of the techniques in this book as you can.

You'll probably fail miserably. Just a heads up. But it will be good for you. You'll learn something. And you'll do better next time. And you'll do even better the time after that.

And eventually, if you use these techniques enough, they'll become habitual. You'll use them instinctually every time you start a new conversation. And people will love you.

It's really not that hard to impress people. You just have to get out of your own head and look at things from their point of view. You have to focus entirely on them. And as you do so, you'll allow yourself to be a better friend than they ever could've imagined. They'll love you forever.

So yeah. You're welcome.

And thanks for taking the time to read this book. You have no idea how much I appreciate you. My life would be horrible without awesome readers like you.

Keep being awesome. You're on the right track. Keep it up.

Peace out my bros.

Made in United States
Orlando, FL
08 March 2022

15561795R00020